MARRIAGE CHALLENGES
for Him 2

One Year of Weekly Suggestions to Love Your
Wife More Effectively and Transform Your Marriage

MANDY SHROCK

Library of Congress Control Number: 2024923501
ISBN: 978-1-958477-17-5 (Paperback)
ISBN: 978-1-958477-18-2 (Digital Online)

Cover and Interior Design by KUHN Design Group | kuhndesigngroup.com

First printing edition 2024

Published by In Abundance, LLC

info@marriageinabundance.com

CONTENTS

FOREWORD

This book of suggested marriage challenges is just "one part of a whole" for Marriage In Abundance's approach to a better marriage. Our goal at Marriage In Abundance is to help couples discover just how deep and meaningful their marriage relationship can be. For best results, this book, along with *Marriage Challenges for Her 2,* is to be used in conjunction with *Marriage In Abundance's Date Plans for Married Couples 2* and *Devotions for Married Couples 2.* To find access to the full program, visit www.marriageinabundance.com.

Here's an overview of what you'll find through Marriage In Abundance:

- **Date Plans for Married Couples**—weekly date plans for fostering creative, engaging, quality time together.

- **Couples' Devotions**—weekly studies to deepen your spiritual connection with God and each other.

- **Marriage Challenges**—weekly suggestions for showing love to one another more effectively, plus monthly suggestions for eliminating unhealthy styles of conflict resolution. As our schedules become overloaded, marital connection takes a backseat. The marriage challenges bring intentionality to meeting one another's needs and desires and spicing up the romance.

INTRODUCTION

WHAT ARE MARRIAGE CHALLENGES?

Sometimes, in trying to meet all of life's demands, connection with our spouse takes a backseat. We fall into a routine that feels more like roommates than lovers. Unless we're intentional about keeping the connection and romance alive, the spark will dwindle. Completing the weekly marriage challenges is a way to be intentional about expressing your love for your wife amid the hustle and bustle and keeping the romance alive.

We all have different needs, desires, and ways we feel loved. Maybe hugs don't mean much to you, but her encouragement does. Maybe a gift feels meaningless compared to her showing interest in you sexually. Typically, when we express love to one another, we do so in a way we understand it, not the way someone else understands it. In trying to make our wives feel loved, we sometimes "miss the mark." Since marriage challenges touch on every avenue of showing love, if you follow our suggestions, you're sure to express love in a way your wife understands. You may even discover a new way she feels love that neither of you knew before!

In addition to the weekly challenges, which are fun ways to show affection, the once-a-month habit reformation challenges will transform your approach to conflict resolution. If you only add fun to the marriage, but don't eliminate the unhealthy habits—such as yelling, interrupting, manipulating, and name-calling—you won't experience as much growth in the marriage. As old habits die hard, you will have one month to focus on better conflict resolution before moving on to another challenge.

MARRIAGE CHALLENGE INSTRUCTIONS

Separate or Together: Most of the challenges are to be done for each other separately. For example, one week you might be challenged to give her a massage with no strings attached, while your wife is challenged to encourage you in an area you are having success. However, sometimes the challenges are to be done together. For example, be intentional about kissing every day that week. In this case, the challenge will say "together," and you can discuss and complete that challenge together. If it doesn't say "together," don't discuss your challenge, just do it.

No Peeping: It is important to keep your challenges in a place your spouse won't be peeping. We don't recommend spouses hide *anything* from each other *ever*—except for the marriage challenges. If your wife sees your challenge and you have not done it, this sets her up for disappointment and will do more harm than good. If you happen to see her challenge lying around, no snooping! Keep your mind focused on your own challenge.

Romance During Everyday Routine: The challenges can be done at any point that is convenient for you that week. However, if you are also participating in the date plans, the challenges are not meant to be done at the same time as the date. The purpose of the marriage challenges is to add intention and romance into your everyday routines, not just on your date together.

A Way to Remember: Part of the problem in keeping the romance alive in a marriage is that you aren't thinking about romance in your everyday lives. It happens to everyone. When you were dating, you were infatuated—smitten—and spent more time thinking about ways you could express love to her. But after you sealed the deal and fell into busyness, you no longer put as much thought into romance. Remembering to pick up this book each week may prove to be just as difficult. So, we suggest setting a couple alarms on your phone—one alarm to remind yourself to pick up your book and look at your challenge for the week, and a second alarm for a time you can complete your challenge that week.

Explicit Content: Considering the marriage challenge's intent is to reignite the romance, some of the challenges, or "assignments," are sexual in nature. Therefore, it is not recommended to keep your marriage challenge books in a place easily accessible to your children.

If any of the sexual marriage challenges cause friction, or trigger a negative emotional response, skip that challenge and prayerfully consider whether there's a deeper issue that needs addressed in counseling.

Stretch and Grow: You may not feel like doing some challenges—not because it triggers a negative emotion, but because it's just not "your thing." For example, maybe you're not into dancing but your challenge is to squeeze in a slow dance after dinner on your living room floor. If you don't do your challenge simply because that's not "your thing," you are limiting growth and denying your spouse full enjoyment of you. Comfort zones are confining. You won't grow if you're not willing to stretch.

Fifth Week: There are four challenges each month. Since there is a fifth week every three months, to stay in the habit, we suggest going back and doing one you missed or doing your favorite again.

Stay Positive: When your spouse does, or says, something nice, you may think, *I bet that was her challenge this week. She only did that because she was told to do it.* Another way to look at it is, *I'm so glad my wife wants to show me love and is giving this a try!*

Make It a Lifestyle: Although the intent is for you to focus on completing one challenge per week, our hope is that, as you begin putting them into practice, these expressions of love become a part of your marriage lifestyle.

JANUARY

Much of the time, when we see our spouse doing something we don't like, we automatically spew out our thoughts and opinions. This can feel like nitpicking. Try to not be quick to spew out negativity. If there's something that really needs addressed, wait for a quiet moment and bring it up gently. You might find it really wasn't that important after all.

(Together) Every day this week, put down your phones and focus solely on each other for fifteen minutes. Use this time to connect about your day, your struggles, and successes. Extra credit: Go for one hour each day.

Ask for her input and advice about
a decision that doesn't involve
her. This makes her feel valued.

Give her an unexpected massage
with no strings attached.

One day this week, when you
sit down to eat dinner, set a few
candles on the table and dim the
lights. (Yes, even if kids are around.)
Tell her you just want to squeeze
in a little romance where you can.

FEBRUARY

Offer grace. Rather than jumping
to conclusions about her intent,
give her the benefit of the doubt.

Write her a note telling her when you started falling for her. Recall the details from the early days of your relationship. Close the letter by assuring her of your positive outlook on your future together.

Let her sleep in one day this week while you prepare her a nice breakfast to wake up to.

Clean the toilet (or do her least favorite chore) before she does.

After you climax, continue pleasuring her. Try to give her multiples, if possible.

MARCH

We often try to make our spouse do things the way *we* would do them. But opposites attract for a reason. Don't try to change her ways. Allow her to be your opposite.

Be intentional about showing physical affection every day this week: hold hands, hug, snuggle, stroke her arms, rub her thighs, run your hands through her hair, etc.

Compliment her appearance.
Not just, "You look good,"
but be specific about what
looks good and why.

Give her neck some
attention with your lips.

Take a selfie as you kiss her on
her cheek. Send it to her.

APRIL

During conflicts, try sandwiching anything that could come across negatively with positive comments. For example, "I love how committed you are in this marriage and how much you support me, but when you put me down in front of others, it's degrading to me. If you have criticisms about me, I would rather you bring them up in private. I do appreciate all the ways you make me a better person."

(Together) Try something new in bed. If you need ideas, try reading the books, *Intended For Pleasure: Sex Technique and Sexual Fulfillment in Christian Marriage,* by Ed Wheat, M.D. and Gaye Wheat or, *Sheet Music: Uncovering the Secrets of Sexual Intimacy in Marriage,* by Dr. Kevin Leman (Chapter 10, specifically).

Encourage her to go out
one night for a girls' night.
Extra credit: Plan it for her!

Write a note telling her how much you love her and that you are praying for her. Stick it in her wallet. (Don't forget to pray for her).

Sacrifice something for her—
maybe your time or energy.
Or give up something you want
for what she wants: the house
temperature, your TV show for
hers, or a habit of yours she hates.

MAY

Let go of your need to "be right."

Tell your kids, a friend, or a family member how much you love your wife (when she's in earshot).

Pray you will see where you
can improve as a husband.

Give her a facial or a scalp
massage. Watch an online tutorial
to learn how to give a good one.

Think about what makes
your wife happy. Encourage
her to pursue that further.

JUNE

(Together) Remember you are a team, not competitors. This means respecting one another's differences and using those differences to move your team forward, cheering your spouse on, and defending your spouse against attacks. Focus on winning together as a team instead of winning as individuals. When in a disagreement, ask yourselves, *How can we win this together?*

(Together) Squeeze in a little extra time with each other this week by doing a routine task together. Ideas: cooking, getting groceries, exercising, or eating lunch.

Think about all that your wife juggles in a day. Thank her for taking care of each of those details and tell her what a good job she's doing.

Take your wife's picture. Typically, women are the picture takers, and no one thinks to take pictures of them. Sneak in a shot when she's laughing with friends or interacting with the kids. Have her pose for a pic when you're on a date. Make sure to send them to her.

Next time you see her frazzled or hurrying, ask her how you can help.

JULY

When disagreeing, be careful that your tone and words don't make your wife feel attacked. Express to her through your tone and words that you care about her and you're in this life—with all its struggles—together with her.

(Together) Passionate kissing
usually ends shortly after
marriage. With no sexpectations,
simply kiss for ten minutes.

You may have said in your vows that you would love and cherish her. To *cherish* means to treasure, hold in high regard, appreciate, and treat with tenderness. Think about your last several interactions with your wife. Ask yourself, *Did I "cherish" her?* Let this self-reflection guide your interactions.

The next chunk of time you would be spending on your hobby, instead, spend time with her.

Kiss her hello and goodbye every day this week. (Extra credit: Tilt her chin up, run your thumb along her lips, then hold the sides of her face as you kiss her.)

AUGUST

Every time a negative thought about your wife comes to mind, replace it with a positive thought about her. What we let our thoughts linger on becomes our predominant view. Allow your view to make a positive shift.

Speak romantically to her during physical intimacy. Ideas: You are amazing; you make me feel like a man; I love you so much; you are the only one for me, etc.

Tell her she is the best thing
that ever happened to you.

Hold her in bed without
sexpectations or touching
her in a sexual way.

Make chocolate covered strawberries for her. If you don't know how, find instructions online.

SEPTEMBER

Don't criticize your wife publicly.

(Together) Make love at a different time of day than you typically do. You may find you prefer the morning before work or a nooner. Experiment and find out.

Whisk her off for a spontaneous dance in your kitchen or living room. Also, make sure your lips get some contact with her ear and neck.

Buy her a random gift based on her interest. It doesn't have to break the bank. Ideas: a picture of something she loves on: socks, a travel mug, a mouse pad, or a key chain.

Post a picture of your spouse on social media and say, "Love this woman," or "Grateful for all my wife does for us," or any other encouragement that comes to mind. If you don't use social media, make it known publicly in another creative way.

OCTOBER

Avoid gunny sacking, which
is keeping a mental list of
grievances, letting them build,
and then pulling them all out
at one time. Stick to resolving
only one issue at a time.

(Together) Go to church this week. During worship, put your arms around each other's waists to acknowledge two things: your marriage is God's gift to you and you're giving your marriage back to God.

Buy her a bouquet with a variety
of flowers. Deem each flower
as a representation of each one
of her wonderful qualities.

Notice something positive about
your wife—her appearance
or something she does well.
Compliment her for it.

Check something off the honey-do list. If you don't have one, ask your wife what needs done or fixed in the home. Make sure to clean up your tools immediately afterward.

NOVEMBER

Stop looking at porn. Although it might not make sense to you, when you look at porn, it makes your wife feel like she's not enough. Not only that, the porn industry is linked to sex-trafficking. End it. We suggest seeking out an accountability partner and installing an accountability app on your phone and every computer.

Make a list of all the things your wife does for you. Tell her you're thankful for all she does and then list out each thing, so she knows you notice and appreciate her. This can be expressed verbally, through text, or in a love note.

Reach for her hand the next time you're walking together.

Ask your wife what's her favorite Scripture or inspirational quote. Make something, or have something made for her, with those words. Ideas: plaque, bookmark, mug, bag, or bracelet.

(Together) Hang mistletoe in your house. Every time you find yourselves under it, you know what to do!

DECEMBER

Depression negatively impacts marriage. If you struggle with depression, seek outside help. This might mean counseling, supplements, or prescription drugs for a chemical imbalance.

Thank God each day this week for a different trait in your wife. (This does not have to be out loud in her presence. Simple gratitude will shift your focus in a positive direction.)

Improve your listening skills. For fifteen minutes each day, focus only on her. Listen without giving advice. Ask questions. Say, "Tell me more about that."

Make her a bath, then tell
her to relax in it while you
put the kids to bed.

This week, every time she does dishes, find another way to help around the house—maybe wipe the countertops, sweep the floor, or pick up toys.

CONCLUSION

We hope you were able to find new ways to express love to each other and were brought closer together on this journey of marriage challenges. If you haven't already, consider participating in the full package of Marriage In Abundance, including date plans and couples' devotions. Find out how by visiting www.marriageinabundance.com. Stay tuned as there will be a third book with another year of fun and bonding activities coming soon!

ABOUT THE AUTHOR

Mandy Shrock is the founder of Marriage In Abundance, a ministry aimed at deepening the bonds of married couples. In addition to writing materials for marriage improvement, she also wrote, *Life In Abundance,* devotions for anyone, no matter their stage in life. She is passionate about life, the Word of God, marriage, sci-fi and fantasy books, exercise, the outdoors, natural foods, and dogs. Powered by coffee, she lives with her husband, four children, and two dogs in northern Indiana.